TIGER SCHMYGER
Educare Books for Young Readers

To Russell, my family, friends, and my fellow Neural Educators for always encouraging and cheering me on and especially all the students who have learned to manage their dinosaur brains

Copyright © Dani Hylton 2023
All Rights Reserved.

Names:	Hylton, Dani, author.
Title:	Sam's dinosaur brain / Dani Hylton.
Description:	Seattle [Washington] : Tiger Schmiger, an imprint of Educare Press Children's Books, [2023]	Series: Brain-based series.
Identifiers: ISBN:	978-0-944638-62-0 (trade)	978-0-944638-56-9 (ebook)
Subjects: LCSH:	Amygdaloid body--Psychological aspects--Juvenile fiction.	Emotional problems of children--Juvenile fiction.	Emotions--Juvenile fiction.	Self-control in children--Juvenile fiction.	Children with disabilities--Education.	Counseling in special education.	Behavior modification.	Teaching--Aids and devices.	CYAC: Brain--Fiction.	Emotional problems-- Fiction.	Emotions--Fiction.	Self-control--Fiction.	BISAC: EDUCATION / General.	EDUCATION / Administration / Elementary & Secondary.	EDUCATION / Behavioral Management.	EDUCATION / Classroom Management.	EDUCATION / Counseling / General.	EDUCATION / Counseling / Crisis Management.	EDUCATION / Educational Psychology.	EDUCATION / Special Education / General.	EDUCATION / Special Education / Behavioral, Emotional & Social Disabilities.	EDUCATION / Special Education / Developmental & Intellectual Disabilities.	EDUCATION / Teacher Training & Certification.
Classification: LCC:	PZ7.1.H934 S36 2023	DDC: [Fic]--dc23

I like to be with my friends

I like to walk my dog

I like to be silly

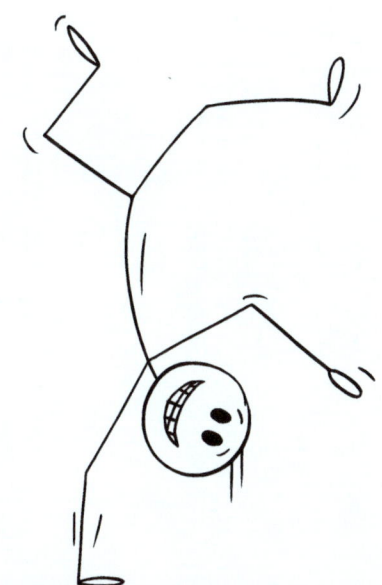

I have a dinosaur brain!

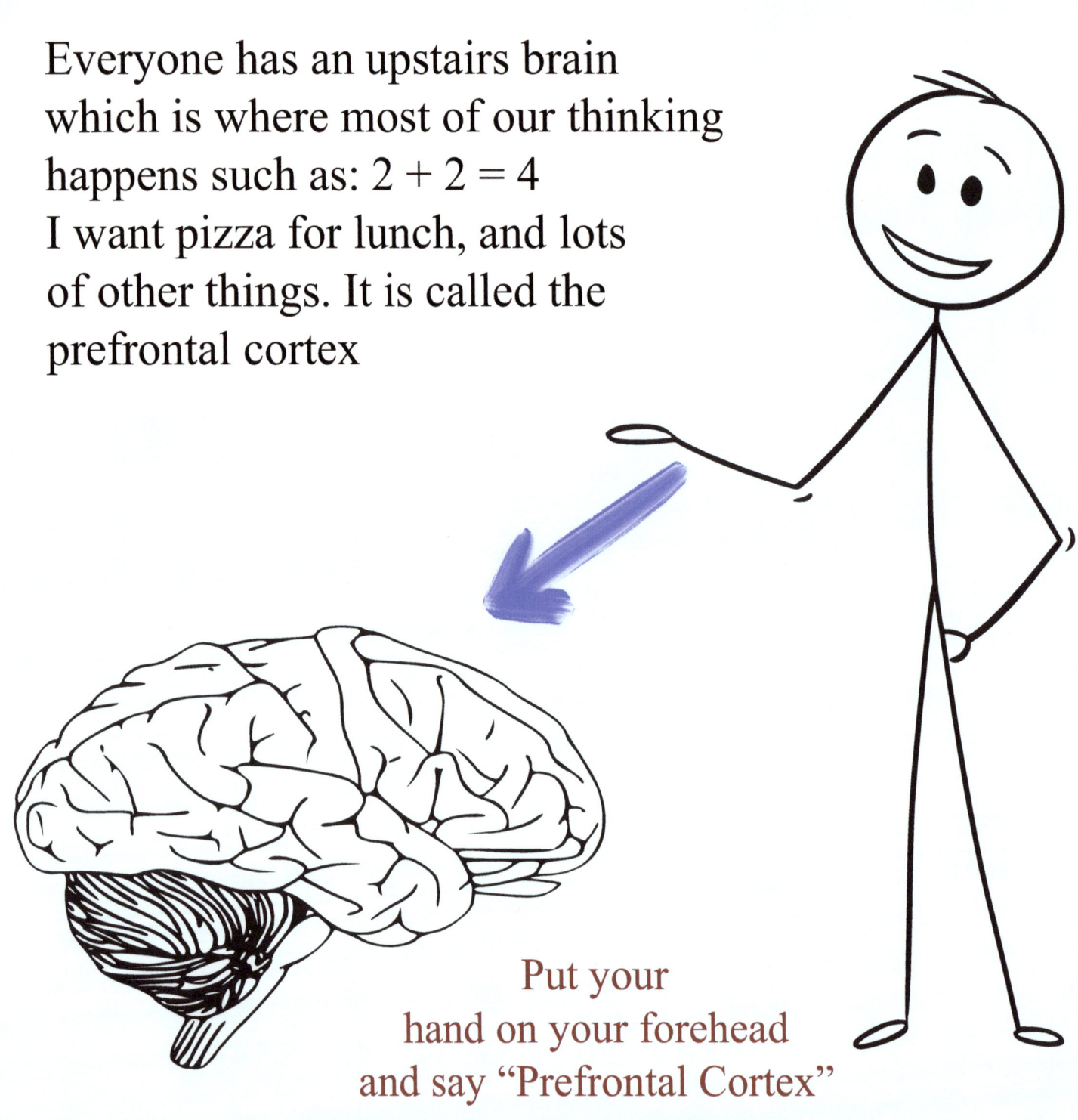

Our downstairs brain handles things that are automatic such as breathing and heartbeat but it also tries to keep us safe from harm.

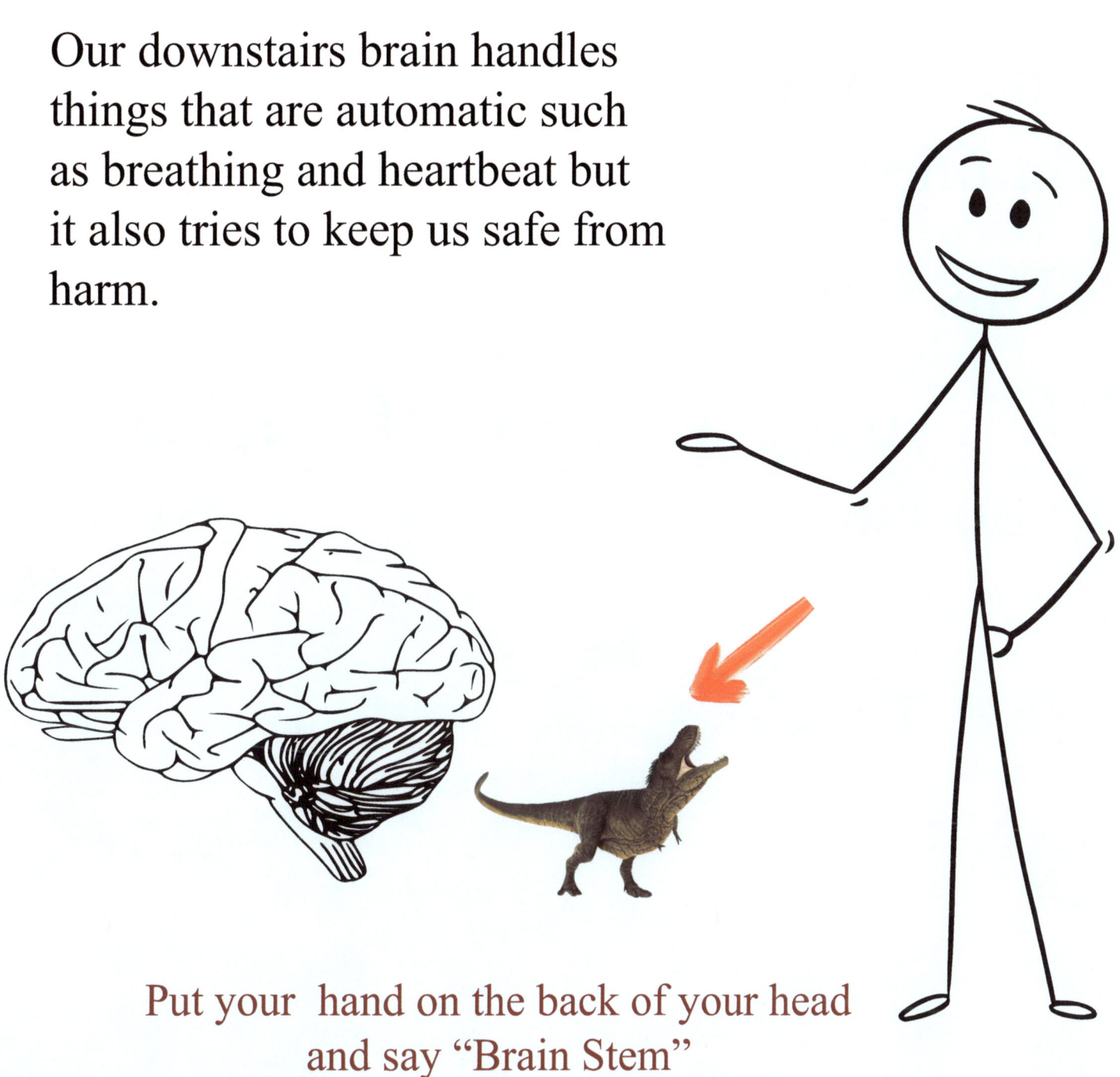

Put your hand on the back of your head and say "Brain Stem"

When something happens that makes you feel scared your brain switches downstairs.

This is your dinosaur brain.

It is your brain's way of keeping you safe.

Your dinosaur brain only has four responses

fight

freeze

fawn ... attempts to please the person who is a threat

flight

If your amygdala is tired, or sad, or hungry… it can Turn-On your dinosaur brain for things that are not dangerous or threatening….

Like when...

I missed the goal

My schoolwork is too hard

no one listens to me

I am bored
I do not know what to do

my friend says mean things

When my brain thinks I am in danger, but I am not… it is called an "**Amygdala Hijack**". This means I only have four responses: fight, flight, freeze or fawn. So, I may do things that are not appropriate for the situation I am in.

When I feel myself switching to my dinosaur brain…

I can take a break or walk away.

Because when I feel like a dinosaur I cannot make good choices

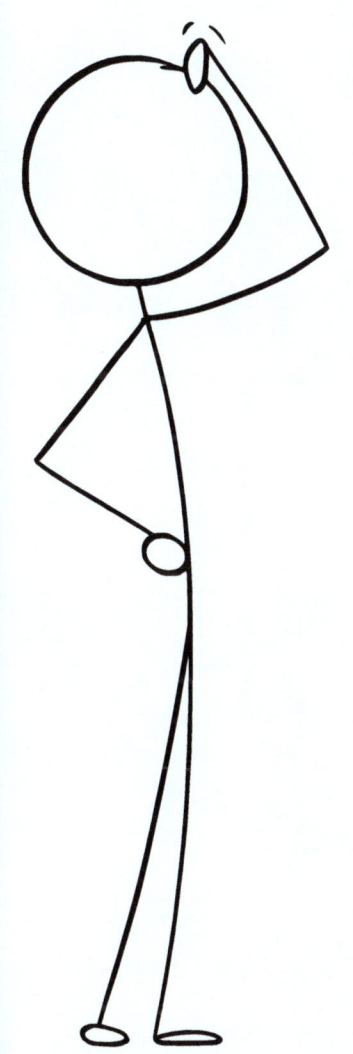

Taking a break or walking away allows me time to process my big feelings and get back into my thinking brain. That is my Prefrontal Cortex.

When I walk away or take a break, I control my dinosaur brain rather than letting it control me.

The End

Teacher Talk

It was Friday afternoon. I was called to a third-grade classroom.

I could see that Lucy was very upset. It took about seventeen minutes for Lucy to calm down.

When she was calm, I read this story to her. And we discussed her dinosaur brain.

On Monday I was again called to Lucy's classroom. She again was very upset.

Next Day: Co-Regulation

This time it took her about fifteen minutes to calm down. When she was finally calm, she looked at me. She sighed and said, "Mrs. Hylton, my dinosaur brain got the best of me."

I agreed with her. We talked a little. How about next time… go to a safe place when you feel your dinosaur brain turning on.

Third Day: Self-Regulation

Tuesday, I received a phone call from her teacher who told me Lucy had asked to come to her safe place because her dinosaur brain was "Turning-On". I hadn't imagined that I would be part of her safe place.

When she arrived, she looked very tense. I let her be. She looked at the fish tank… wandered about a bit. And then…

She came over and said, "Mrs. Hylton I feel better now… my dinosaur brain was turning on. I just needed to take a break."

www.ingramcontent.com/pod-product-compliance
Lightning Source LLC
Chambersburg PA
CBHW042144290426

44110CB00002B/111